Little Piano

Fun, Easy, Step-By-Step, Teach-Yourself Song and Beginner Piano Guide (Book & Streaming Videos)

New Edition with Bonus Lessons!

Book & Streaming Videos by Damon Ferrante

Introduction

How the Book & Videos Work

The Book

As a piano professor and piano teacher for over 25 years, I have designed this book and video course to follow a step-by-step lesson format for learning how to play the piano. It is designed for beginners and no music experience is necessary to use the book. Each lesson builds on the previous one in a clear and easy-to-understand manner. You will learn how to play the piano and learn how to read music through studying famous songs and pieces. At the end of this new edition, there are lessons to guide you through basic piano technique.

At the end of the book, you will be able to play the following songs and pieces in easy-piano arrangements: *Jingle Bells, Scarborough Fair, Ode to Joy, Amazing Grace, When the Saints Go Marching In, Yankee Doodle, Simple Gifts, Take Me Out to the Ballgame, Michael, Row the Boat Ashore, Beethoven 5th Symphony Theme, Twinkle, Twinkle Little Star, Love Somebody, Kum-Bah-Yah,* and many more songs.

The Videos

There are 10 Free, Streaming Video Lessons that coincide with the material presented in *The Little Piano Book.* The Lesson Videos cover playing songs and pieces, piano technique, how to read music, and basic music elements and fundamentals. All of these videos are <u>free</u>. To access the videos, go to <u>SteeplechaseMusic.com</u> and click on the link for Piano Books at top of the Home Page. Then, on the Piano Books Page, click on the cover image for the *Little Piano Book.* On the webpage for the *Little Piano Book,* you will see a link / image for the video lessons. Click on the link / image for access. You may also type the webpage address into the browser window of your computer or device, for another easy way to access the videos:

http://www.steeplechasemusic.com/video-lessons2.html

Table of Contents

Steeplechase Music Books

Also by Damon Ferrante

Piano Scales, Chords & Arpeggios Lessons with Elements of Basic Music Theory: Fun, Step-By-Step Guide for Beginner to Advanced Levels (Book & Videos)

Guitar Adventures: Fun, Step-By-Step Guide to Beginner Guitar (Book & Videos)

Guitar Scales Handbook: A Step-By-Step, 100-Lesson Guide to Scales, Music Theory, and Fretboard Theory (Book & Videos)

Guitar Adventures for Kids: Fun, Step-By-Step, Beginner Lesson Guide to Get You Started (Book & Videos)

Beginner Rock Guitar Lessons: Instruction Guide (Book & Videos)

Ultimate Guitar Chords, Scales & Arpeggios Handbook: 240-Lesson, Step-By-Step Guitar Guide, Beginner to Advanced Levels (Book & Videos)

Little Piano Book: Fun, Easy, Step-By-Step, Teach-Yourself Song and Beginner Piano Guide (Book & Streaming Videos)

by Damon Ferrante

For additional information about music books, recordings, and concerts, please visit the Steeplechase website: www.steeplechasemusic.com

steepLechase

arts & productions

ISBN-13:
978-0615874296 (Steeplechase Arts) / ISBN-10: 0615874290

Right Hand

Chapter 1

Lesson 1: Hand Position & Finger Numbers

- To create a good hand position for piano playing is easy. With both hands, imagine that you are holding an apple (with your palms facing upward and your fingers curved). Then, turn your palms to the floor and keep your fingers curved. **See Video Lesson 1**
- For piano playing, our fingers are given numbers. The numbers are the same for both hands. **See Video Lesson 1**

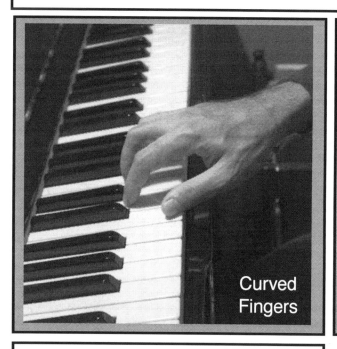

Curved Fingers

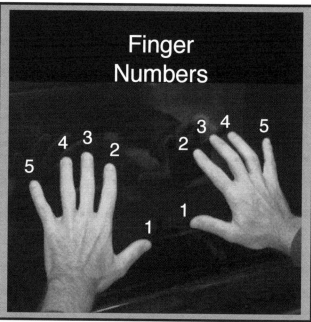

Finger Numbers

- RH stands for Right Hand.
- LH stands for Left Hand.

Finger Numbers
- Thumb = Finger #1
- Pointer = Finger #2
- Middle = Finger #3
- Ring = Finger #4
- Pinky = Finger #5

The finger numbers are the same for both hands. For example, the thumb is finger #1 in both the right hand and left hand and the pinky is finger #5 in both hands.

For Video Lesson 1, go to www.steeplechasemusic.com.

Lesson 2: Middle C & Good Posture at the Piano

- On the Piano Keyboard, you might notice that there are 2 sets of keys: Black and White Keys. The Black Keys are in groups of 2 and 3 keys.
- If you look near the middle of the piano keyboard, you will see a set of 2 Black Keys. The White Key, directly to the Left of this set of 2 Black Keys (near the middle of the piano keyboard) is called "Middle C".
- Middle C is an important reference note on the piano. We will be playing it in many of our songs.
- For some help in locating Middle C on the piano, **See Video Lesson 1.**

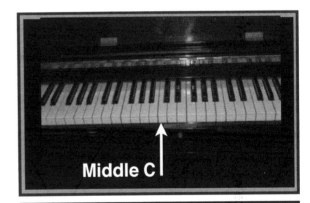

Middle C

From the beginning of your piano playing, it is important to practice good posture: keep your back straight and your arms and shoulders relaxed.

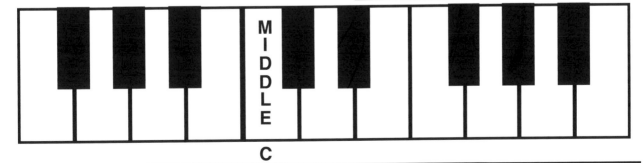

M
I
D
D
L
E

C

Exercises:
- Try Locating Middle C with Finger #1 (Thumb) of your Right Hand (RH)
- Try Locating Middle C with Finger #1 (Thumb) of your Left Hand (LH)

Lesson 3: Keyboard Notes

- The White Keys on the piano follow an alphabetic pattern that goes from A to G. In other words, this is the pattern: A, B, C, D, E, F, G.
- This pattern starts at the bottom (low bass notes) of the piano keyboard and repeats many times as the notes go upward and get higher in pitch ("sound").
- With your RH ("Right Hand") Index Finger, find the "A" key just 2 keys below MIddle C (See the Chart below). Move your Index Finger up (to the right) one key at a time. Try saying the letters as you press down each key. **See Video Lesson 1**

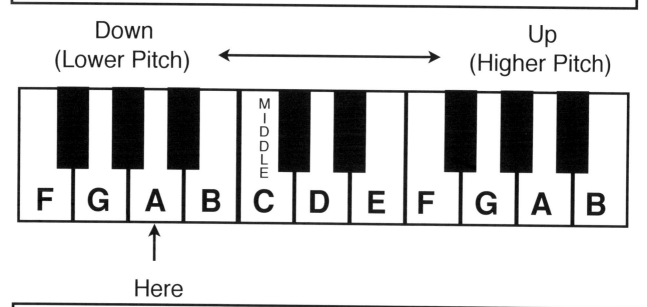

- It is a good idea to associate each key with some object and imagine the object on top of the key. This will help you remember the name and location of each key.
- For this exercise, let's image that the piano keyboard is a table with food on it. The food, on this imagined table, will be placed in a set order going from left to right (See the chart below). Find the key "A" below Middle C and name the foods as you move upward (right). When you get to the second key "A", the pattern will repeat. Repeat this exercise.

White Keys Exercise: A= Apple, B= Bread, C= Cheese, D= Dessert, E= Eggs, F= Fish, G= Grapes

Exercises:
- Try Locating Middle C with Finger #1 (Thumb) of your Right Hand (RH)
- Try Locating Middle C with Finger #1 (Thumb) of your Left Hand (LH)
- Try Locating D with Finger #2 (Pointer Finger) of your Right Hand (RH)
- Try Locating E with Finger #3 (Middle Finger) of your Right Hand (RH)
- Try Locating G with Finger #5 (Pinky Finger) of your Right Hand (RH)

Lesson 4: Three-Note Songs, Using the Right Hand ("RH")

- Try these songs, which use the notes C, D, and E in the right hand ("RH").
- In your right hand, use Thumb for Middle C, use Pointer for D, and use Middle Finger for E.
- Take a look at the keyboard chart and photo below and practice each song 5-10 times.
- As an extra bonus, try saying the letter names aloud as you play each song. This will help you associate the note name with the key and finger number.

Notes:
Finger Numbers:

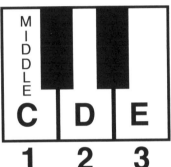

C, D, and E in
the Right Hand

Springtime

| RH: 1 1 1 1 | 2 2 2 2 | 3 3 3 3 | 2 2 1 1 |
| C C C C | D D D D | E E E E | D D C C |

Dancing

| RH: 1 1 2 2 | 1 1 3 3 | 1 1 2 2 | 1 1 1 1 |
| C C D D | C C E E | C C D D | C C C C |

Lesson 5: More Three-Note Songs Using the Right Hand

• Try these songs, which also use the notes C, D, and E in the right hand ("RH").

RH

Notes: **C D E**

Finger Numbers: **1 2 3**

Try saying the notes aloud as you play each song.

The double lines (called the "Double Bar") indicate the end of a song or piece.

Jazz Dance

RH: 2 2 1 1 | 2 2 3 3 | 2 2 1 2 | 2 2 1 2 ‖
D D C C | D D E E | D D C D | D D C D

Blue Sky

RH: 3 2 3 1 | 2 2 2 2 | 3 2 3 1 | 2 2 1 1 ‖
E D E C | D D D D | E D E C | D D C C

Soccer Fun

RH: 1 1 3 3 | 2 2 3 3 | 1 1 3 3 | 2 2 1 1 ‖
C C E E | D D E E | C C E E | D D C C

Lesson 6: Counting & Measures

- Music is composed of groups of beats called measures.
- Measures are set off by vertical lines, called bar lines.
- Measures most commonly contain 2, 3, or 4 beats.
- Below, are examples of sets of four measures in 4/4 time.
- In 4/4 time, you will count 4 beats for each measure.
  In other words, you will count: 1234, 1234, 1234, 1234.
- Try counting aloud and clapping the beats for the exercise below.

See Video
Lesson 2

Example 1:

| 1 2 3 4 | 1 2 3 4 | 1 2 3 4 | 1 2 3 4 ‖

Example 2:
Try Clapping on the X: On the First Beat.

| 1 2 3 4 | 1 2 3 4 | 1 2 3 4 | 1 2 3 4 ‖
  X   X   X   X

Example 3:
Try Clapping on the X: On the First and Third Beats.

| 1 2 3 4 | 1 2 3 4 | 1 2 3 4 | 1 2 3 4 ‖
  X   X   X   X   X   X   X   X

Example 4:
Try Clapping on the X: On the Second Beat.

| 1 2 3 4 | 1 2 3 4 | 1 2 3 4 | 1 2 3 4 ‖
    X   X   X   X

Lesson 7: Counting along with Three-Note Songs (RH)

- Try counting aloud (1234) for each measure, while playing these songs. The songs use the notes C, D, and E in the right hand ("RH"): Fingers 1, 2, and 3. *Have fun!*

RH

Notes:

C   D   E

Finger Numbers: **1**   **2**   **3**

*The Numbers in these songs are for the <u>Beats</u>, <u>not</u> the Finger Numbers.

Summer Rock

Beats:	1 2 3 4	1 2 3 4	1 2 3 4	1 2 3 4
	D D C D	D D C D	E E D D	E E D D

A Short Walk

Beats:	1 2 3 4	1 2 3 4	1 2 3 4	1 2 3 4
	C C C C	D D D D	E E D D	C C C C

When's Dessert?

Beats:	1 2 3 4	1 2 3 4	1 2 3 4	1 2 3 4
	E D C C	D D E E	D D C D	E D C C

Lesson 8: 5-Note Songs
Right Hand (RH)

- Let's add 2 new notes for the right hand ("RH"): F and G.
- F will be played with the 4th finger (Ring Finger).
- G will be played with the 5th finger (Pinky Finger).

RH

Notes: **C D E F G**

Finger Numbers: **1 2 3 4 5**

New Notes

The numbers here are for <u>beats</u>, not fingers. When there is a blank space, don't play for that beat or beats.

Mary's Little Lamb

Beats:	1	2	3	4		1	2	3	4		1	2	3	4		1	2	3	4
	E	D	C	D		E	E	E			D	D	D			E	G	G	
	Ma-	ry	had	a		lit-	tle	lamb,			lit-	tle	lamb,			lit-	tle	lamb.	

Jingle Bells

Beats:	1	2	3	4		1	2	3	4		1	2	3	4		1	2	3	4
	E	E	E			E	E	E			E	G	C	D		E			
	Jin-	gle	Bells,			Jin-	gle	Bells,			Jin-	gle	all	the		way.			

Beats:	1	2	3	4		1	2	3	4		1	2	3	4		1	2	3	4
	F	F	F	F		F	E	E	E		E	D	D	E		D		G	
	Oh!	What	fun	it		is	to	ride	in		a	one-horse	open			sleigh!		Hey!	

Lesson 9: More 5-Note Songs for the Right Hand (RH)

> • Here are a few more songs that use the five fingers of the right hand.
> • Remember to find Middle C with the Thumb of your right hand (RH).

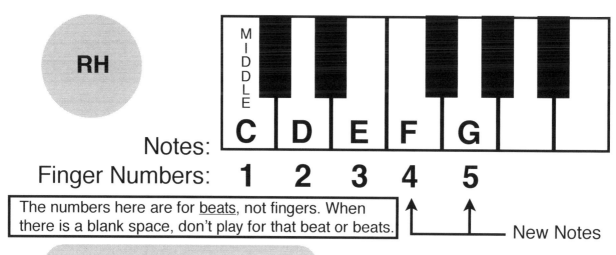

RH

Notes: C D E F G

Finger Numbers: 1 2 3 4 5

> The numbers here are for <u>beats</u>, not fingers. When there is a blank space, don't play for that beat or beats.

New Notes

Starlight

Beats:	1	2	3	4		1	2	3	4		1	2	3	4		1	2	3	4	
	F	E	D	C		G	G	G			F	E	D	C		G	G	C	C	

Ode to Joy

Beats:	1	2	3	4		1	2	3	4		1	2	3	4		1	2	3	4	
	E	E	F	G		G	F	E	D		C	C	D	E		E	D	D		

Beats:	1	2	3	4		1	2	3	4		1	2	3	4		1	2	3	4	
	E	E	F	G		G	F	E	D		C	C	D	E		D	C	C		

Lesson 10: Chapter 1
What We Have Learned

- Finger Numbers: 1, 2, 3, 4, and 5

- Right-Hand & Left-Hand Abbreviations: RH & LH

- Good Piano Technique: Curved Fingers

- Finding Middle C

- Counting and Measures

- Naming the Notes While Playing Songs

- Counting the Beats While Playing Songs

Check Out These Artists, Songs, and Pieces

- Beethoven: *Für Elise*

- Billy Joel: *The Piano Man*

- Ray Charles: *Georgia On My Mind*

- Vanessa Carlton: *A Thousand Miles*

- Chopin: *The Minute Waltz*

Left Hand

Chapter 2

Lesson 11: Three-Note Songs, Using the Left Hand ("LH")

- Try these songs, which use the notes A, B, and Middle C in the left hand ("LH").
- In your left hand, use Thumb for Middle C, use Pointer for B, and use Middle Finger for A.
- Take a look at the keyboard chart and photo below and practice each song 5-10 times.
- As an extra bonus, try saying the letter names aloud as you play each song. This will help you associate the note name with the key and finger number. **Have Fun!**

LH

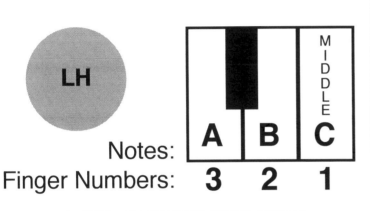

Notes: **A B C** (MIDDLE)

Finger Numbers: **3 2 1**

The numbers here are for <u>fingers</u>, not beats.

A, B, and C in the Left Hand

In Winter

LH:	1 1 2 3	1 1 2 3	2 2 3 3	2 2 3 3
	C C B A	C C B A	B B A A	B B A A

A Mystery

LH:	3 2 1 2	3 2 1 2	1 1 3 3	1 2 3 3
	A B C B	A B C B	C C A A	C B A A

Lesson 12: More Three-Note Songs Using the Left Hand

• Try these songs, which also use the notes A, B, and C in the Left hand ("LH").

LH

Notes: **A B C**   (MIDDLE)

Finger Numbers: **3   2   1**

Try saying the notes aloud as you play each song.

The numbers here are for <u>fingers</u>, not beats.

Moments

LH: **2 3 2 3** | **1 1 1 1** | **2 3 2 3** | **1 1 3 3** ‖
     B A B A | **C C C C** | **B A B A** | **C C A A**

Clouds

LH: **1 3 2 1** | **1 3 2 1** | **2 2 3 3** | **1 2 3 3** ‖
     C A B C | **C A B C** | **B B A A** | **C B A A**

The Storm

LH: **1 3 1 3** | **2 3 2 3** | **1 3 1 3** | **2 2 3 3** ‖
     C A C A | **B A B A** | **C A C A** | **B B A A**

Lesson 13: Time Signatures

- Measures are composed of groups of beats called Time Signatures or Meter (both terms mean the same thing and are interchangeable).
- The most common Time Signatures (or "meters") are groups of 2, 3, or 4 beats per measure: 2/4, 3/4, and 4/4 Time Signatures.
- 2/4 Time Signature groups the notes into measures of 2 beats. Count: "One,Two" for each measure.
- 3/4 Time Signature groups the notes into measures of 3 beats. Count: "One,Two,Three" for each measure.
- 4/4 Time Signature groups the notes into measures of 4 beats. Count: "One,Two,Three, Four" for each measure.
- Below, are examples of sets of four measures in 2/4, 3/4, and 4/4.
- Count aloud and clap on the first beat for the exercises below.

See Video Lesson 3

Example 1: 2/4 Time Signature
Try Clapping on the X: On the First Beat.

$\frac{2}{4}$

| 1 | 2 | | 1 | 2 | | 1 | 2 | | 1 | 2 |
| X | | | X | | | X | | | X | |

Example 2: 3/4 Time Signature
Try Clapping on the X: On the First Beat.

$\frac{3}{4}$

| 1 | 2 | 3 | | 1 | 2 | 3 | | 1 | 2 | 3 | | 1 | 2 | 3 |
| X | | | | X | | | | X | | | | X | | |

Example 3: 4/4 Time Signature
Try Clapping on the X: On the First Beat.

$\frac{4}{4}$

| 1 | 2 | 3 | 4 | | 1 | 2 | 3 | 4 | | 1 | 2 | 3 | 4 | | 1 | 2 | 3 | 4 |
| X | | | | | X | | | | | X | | | | | X | | | |

Lesson 14: Counting along with 3-Note Songs (LH) in 3/4 Time

- Try counting aloud (123) for each measure, while playing these songs. The songs are all in 3/4 Time Signatures (which can also be called "3/4 Time"). The songs use the notes A, B, and C in the left hand ("LH"): Fingers 3, 2, and 1. *Have fun!*

LH

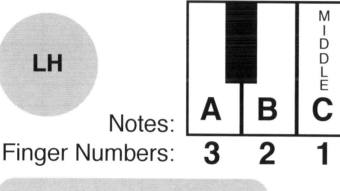

Notes:

Finger Numbers: **3** **2** **1**

See Video Lesson 3

For Video Lesson 3, go to www.steeplechasemusic.com.

***The Numbers in these songs are for the <u>Beats</u>, <u>not</u> the Finger Numbers.**

Waltz in A Minor

3
4

Beats:												
1	2	3	1	2	3	1	2	3	1	2	3
C	A	A	C	A	A	B	A	A	C	A	A

Falling Leaves

3
4

Beats:												
1	2	3	1	2	3	1	2	3	1	2	3
A	B	C	A	B	C	B	A	B	C	B	A

A Memory

3
4

Beats:												
1	2	3	1	2	3	1	2	3	1	2	3
C	B	A	C	C	C	B	B	B	C	B	A

Lesson 15: 5-Note Songs for the Left Hand (LH)

- Let's add 2 new notes for the left hand ("LH"): F and G.
- F will be played with the 5th finger (Pinky Finger).
- G will be played with the 4th finger (Ring Finger).

LH

Notes: **F** **G** **A** **B** **C** (MIDDLE C)

Finger Numbers: **5** **4** **3** **2** **1**

New Notes

- These 2 songs are in 3/4 time (or "time signature").
- Remember to count "One, Two, Three" for each measure.
- The numbers here are for the <u>beats</u>, not the fingers.

Sunny Day

Beats:

$\dfrac{3}{4}$

1	2	3	1	2	3	1	2	3	1	2	3
C	A	F	C	A	F	G	G	C	C	A	F

A Memory

Beats:

$\dfrac{3}{4}$

1	2	3	1	2	3	1	2	3	1	2	3
F	G	A	F	A	C	F	G	A	C	A	F

Lesson 16: More 5-Note Songs for the Left Hand (LH)

- Here are a few more songs that use the five fingers of the left hand.
- Remember to find Middle C with the Thumb of your left hand (LH).

LH

Notes: F G A B C

Finger Numbers: 5 4 3 2 1

These 2 songs are in 4/4 time. Remember to count four beats for each measure. The numbers here are for <u>beats</u>, not fingers.

Cakes

Beats:

| 4 | 1 2 3 4 | 1 2 3 4 | 1 2 3 4 | 1 2 3 4 |
| 4 | F G A G | C C G G | F G A G | C B C C |

Weekend Day Trip

Beats:

| 4 | 1 2 3 4 | 1 2 3 4 | 1 2 3 4 | 1 2 3 4 |
| 4 | C G F G | C G F G | A A C C | G G G G |

| 1 2 3 4 | 1 2 3 4 | 1 2 3 4 | 1 2 3 4 |
| C G F G | C G F G | A A C C | G F F F |

Lesson 17: Chapter 2
What We Have Learned

- Left-Hand Notes: F, G, A, B, and C

- An Introduction to Time Signatures

- Counting and Clapping Time Signatures

- Songs in 3/4 Time

- Left-Hand Piano Technique

- Counting the Beats Aloud While Playing Songs

- Saying the Note Names While Playing Songs

Check Out These Artists, Songs, and Pieces

- Mozart: *The Turkish Rondo*

- Beethoven: *The Moonlight Sonata*

- Bill Evans: *Autumn Leaves*

- Scott Joplin: *The Entertainer*

- Elton John: *Bennie and the Jets*

Both Hands

Chapter 3

Lesson 18: Keyboard Notes, Both Hands: A,B,C,D,E

- Now we will be playing songs that involve both the right and left hands.
- Find Middle C with both your Right and Left-Hand Thumbs.
- For the next few pieces, both Thumbs will share Middle C.
- These first songs will involve 3 fingers for each hand.
- Gradually we will add additional fingers.
- The Letters positioned above the beats are for Right Hand (RH).
- The Letters positioned below the beats are for Left Hand (LH).

See Video Lesson 4

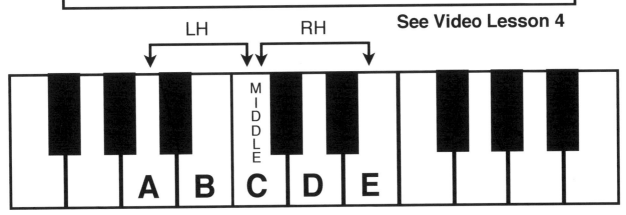

Finger Numbers: **3   2   1   2   3**

Both Thumbs (RH and LH) share Middle C.

*The Numbers in this song are for the <u>Beats</u>, <u>not</u> the Finger Numbers.

Three Kings

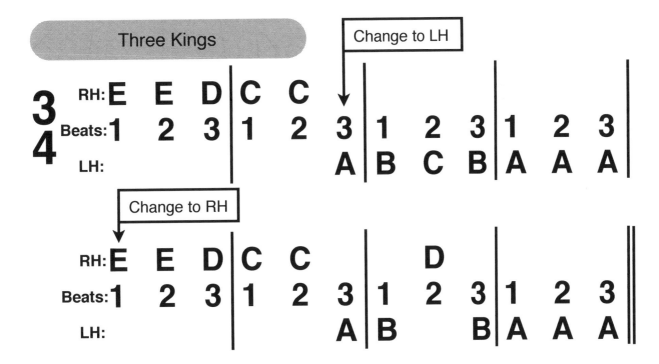

Lesson 19: Keyboard Notes, Both Hands: A,B,C,D,E

- Here are 2 pieces for both hands. They use the notes A, B, C, D, and E.
- The numbers listed are for the <u>beats</u>, not the finger numbers.
- If there is a blank space, don't play for that beat or beats.
- Both Thumbs will share Middle C.

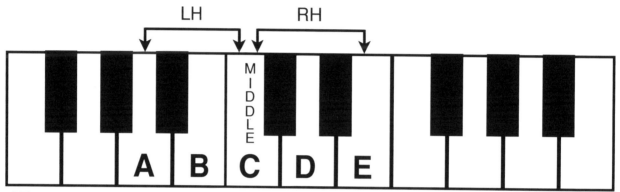

Finger
Numbers: **3   2   1   2   3**
Both Thumbs (RH and LH) share Middle C.

Beethoven 5th Symphony Theme

	RH:	E	E	E	C			D	D	D			
3/4	Beats:	1	2	3	1	2	3	1	2	3	1	2	3
	LH:										B		

What a View!

	RH:	C	D	E	C			C	D	E	G		C
3/4	Beats:	1	2	3	1	2	3	1	2	3	1	2	3
	LH:					G	G						G

Lesson 20: Keyboard Notes, Both Hands: G,A,B,C,D,E,F

- Let's add 2 notes: G in the Left Hand and F in the Right Hand.
- Both of these new notes will be played with the Ring Fingers.

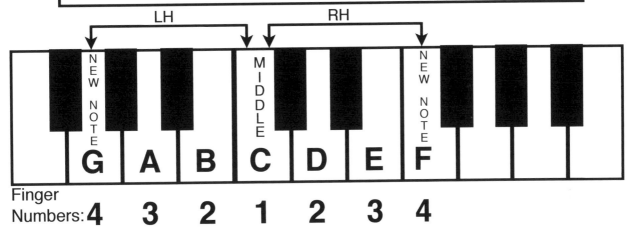

Finger Numbers: **4 3 2 1 2 3 4**

Both Thumbs (RH and LH) share Middle C.

Yankee Doodle

See Video Lesson 4

RH: **C C D E | C E D | C C D E | C**

$\frac{4}{4}$ Beats: **1 2 3 4 | 1 2 3 4 | 1 2 3 4 | 1 2 3 4**

LH: **B**

RH: **C C D E | F E D C | | C C**

Beats: **1 2 3 4 | 1 2 3 4 | 1 2 3 4 | 1 2 3 4**

LH: **B G A B**

March

RH: **C   C | C | C C | C C**

$\frac{4}{4}$ Beats: **1 2 3 4 | 1 2 3 4 | 1 2 3 4 | 1 2 3 4**

LH: **G G | A B G | G G | A B**

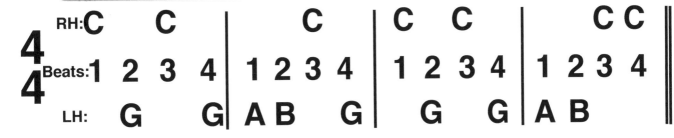

Lesson 21: *Twinkle, Twinkle*
Both Hands: G,A,B,C,D,E,F

• If you see a blank space, don't play for that beat or beats.
• Remember to place both of your thumbs on Middle C.

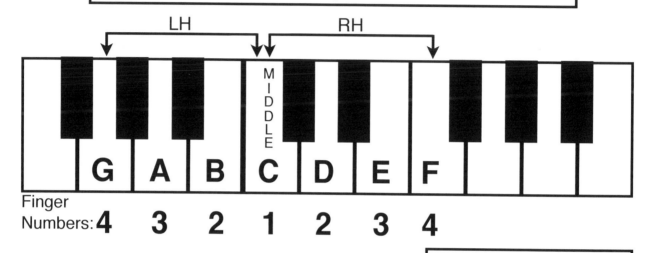

LH   RH

MIDDLE

G	A	B	C	D	E	F

Finger Numbers: 4   3   2   1   2   3   4

• Try to count the beats aloud, while you play.

Twinkle, Twinkle

	Beat 1	Beat 2	Beat 3	Beat 4		Beat 1	Beat 2	Beat 3	Beat 4		Beat 1	Beat 2	Beat 3	Beat 4		Beat 1	Beat 2	Beat 3	Beat 4
RH:		D	D			E	E	D			C	C							
Beats:	1	2	3	4		1	2	3	4		1	2	3	4		1	2	3	4
LH:	G	G											B	B		A	A	G	

	Beat 1	Beat 2	Beat 3	Beat 4		Beat 1	Beat 2	Beat 3	Beat 4		Beat 1	Beat 2	Beat 3	Beat 4		Beat 1	Beat 2	Beat 3	Beat 4
RH:	D	D	C	C							D	D	C	C					
Beats:	1	2	3	4		1	2	3	4		1	2	3	4		1	2	3	4
LH:						B	B	A								B	B	A	

	Beat 1	Beat 2	Beat 3	Beat 4		Beat 1	Beat 2	Beat 3	Beat 4		Beat 1	Beat 2	Beat 3	Beat 4		Beat 1	Beat 2	Beat 3	Beat 4
RH:		D	D			E	E	D			C	C							
Beats:	1	2	3	4		1	2	3	4		1	2	3	4		1	2	3	4
LH:	G	G											B	B		A	A	G	

$\frac{4}{4}$

Lesson 22: *The Ballgame*
Both Hands: F,G,A,B,C,D,E,F,G

- Let's add 1 more note for each hand: "F" in the Left Hand and "G" in the right hand.
- Both for these notes ("F" in LH and "G" in RH) will be played with the 5th finger (Pinky).
- Remember, the numbers in these songs are for the <u>beats</u>, not for the fingers.

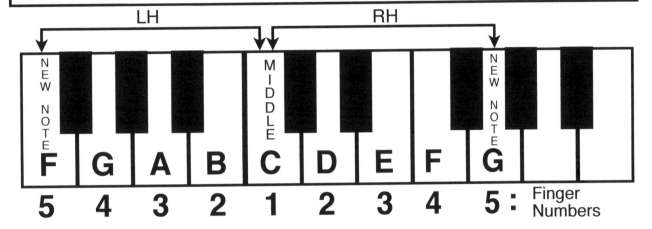

- Both Thumbs (RH and LH) share Middle C for this song.
- If there is a blank space, don't play for that beat or beats. In music, these silent beats are called "Rests. We will learn more about Rests later in this book.
- For "The Ballgame", try to say the note names aloud, as you play the song. This will help you associate the letter names with the keys and will allow to improve faster.

The Ballgame

RH:			F	D	C		C			C		
Beats: 1	2	3	1	2	3	1	2	3	1	2	3
LH: F					A				G		

(Time signature: 3/4)

RH:			F	D	C		C					
Beats: 1	2	3	1	2	3	1	2	3	1	2	3
LH: F					A				C		

Lesson 23: Music Theory: What are Intervals?

- In music, the distance between any 2 notes is called an "Interval".
- Intervals can be played at the same time, for example, if you press down two piano keys or they can be played one after the other, for example, if you play the note "C" and then the note "D".
- On the piano, the easiest way to understand intervals is to look at the keyboard. Play Middle C with your Left-Hand Index Finger, then play D with your Right-Hand Index finger. This interval is called a 2nd.
- Next, play Middle C with your Left-Hand Index Finger, then play E with your Right-Hand Index finger. This interval is called a 3rd.
- Follow these steps in the 2 diagrams below. Use the Left-Hand Index Finger when you see LH and use the Right-Hand Index Finger when you see RH.

See Video Lesson 5

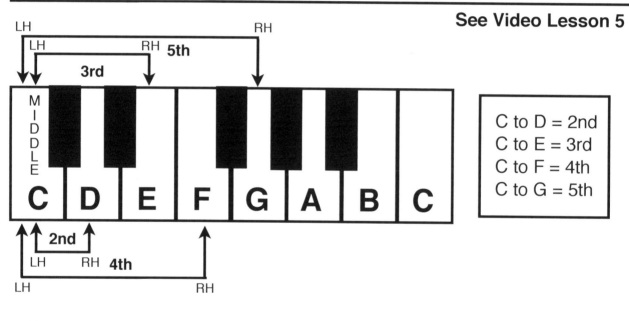

C to D = 2nd
C to E = 3rd
C to F = 4th
C to G = 5th

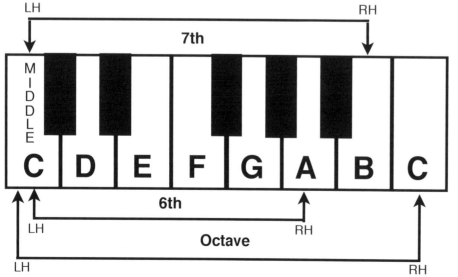

C to A = 6th
C to B = 7th
C to C = Octave

Lesson 24: Both Hands at the Same Time: F,G,A,B,C,D,E,F,G

- In these next songs, we will be playing notes with the Right Hand and Left Hand at the same time.
- When one letter is on top of another letter, play both at the same time. *Have Fun!*

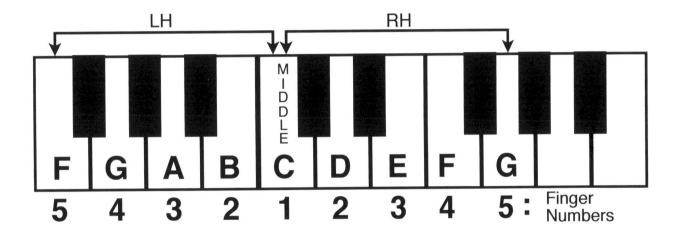

	LH					RH			
	F	G	A	B	C	D	E	F	G
	5	4	3	2	1	2	3	4	5 : Finger Numbers

Fanfare

RH:	G	G	G	G	E	E	E	E	F	F	F	F	E	E	E	E	
Beats:	1	2	3	4	1	2	3	4	1	2	3	4	1	2	3	4	
LH:	C	C	C	C	C	C	C	C	C	C	C	C	C	C	C	C	

$\frac{4}{4}$

RH:	G	G	G	G	E	E	E	E	F	F	F	F	C			
Beats:	1	2	3	4	1	2	3	4	1	2	3	4	1	2	3	4
LH:	C	C	C	C	C	C	C	C	C	C	C	C	G			

Lesson 25: Both Hands at the Same Time: F,G,A,B,C,D,E,F,G

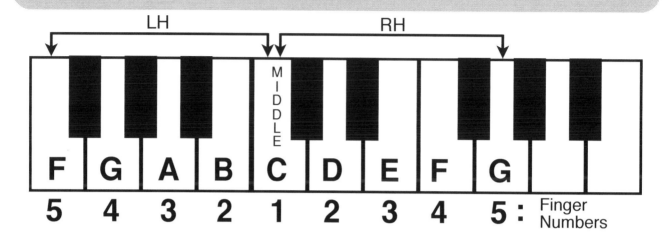

Love Somebody

RH:	C	E	G	G	D	E	F		C	E	G	G	F	E	D	
Beats:	1	2	3	4	1	2	3	4	1	2	3	4	1	2	3	4
LH:	G				G				G				A			

4/4

RH:	C	E	G	G	D	E	F		E	E	D	D	C	C	C	
Beats:	1	2	3	4	1	2	3	4	1	2	3	4	1	2	3	4
LH:	G				G				G				G			

Snow Flurries

RH:	E				E				D	D	D	D	C	C	C	C
Beats:	1	2	3	4	1	2	3	4	1	2	3	4	1	2	3	4
LH:	A	B	C	B	A	B	C	B	B	B	B	B	A	A	A	A

4/4

Lesson 26: Both Hands at the Same Time: F,G,A,B,C,D,E,F,G

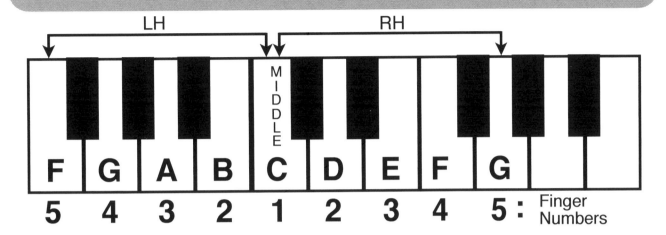

LH   RH

F	G	A	B	C	D	E	F	G	Finger Numbers
5	4	3	2	1	2	3	4	5 :	

MIDDLE

Ode to Joy

Try this more advanced version of Beethoven's *Ode to Joy*.

$\frac{4}{4}$ Beats:

E E F G	G F E D	C C D E	E D D
1 2 3 4	1 2 3 4	1 2 3 4	1 2 3 4
G	C	A	G

E E F G	G F E D	C C D E	D C C
1 2 3 4	1 2 3 4	1 2 3 4	1 2 3 4
G	C	A	G

Summer Evening

$\frac{4}{4}$

RH:	G E	F D	E C	C C
Beats:	1 2 3 4	1 2 3 4	1 2 3 4	1 2 3 4
LH:	C C	B B	A A	G B

Lesson 27: Upbeats & *When the Saints Go Marching In*

- In music, there are many songs and pieces that use Upbeats.
- An Upbeat (or Upbeats) are a note or group of notes that occur before the first full measure of a song or piece of music.
- Upbeats act as very short introductory phrases that emphasize an important note or word at the beginning of a song. For example, in *When the Saints Go Marching In*, the words "Oh when the" are the upbeat. They lead into and accentuate the word "saints".

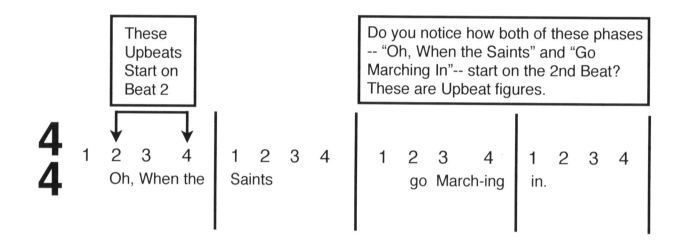

These Upbeats Start on Beat 2

Do you notice how both of these phases -- "Oh, When the Saints" and "Go Marching In"-- start on the 2nd Beat? These are Upbeat figures.

When the Saints Go Marching In

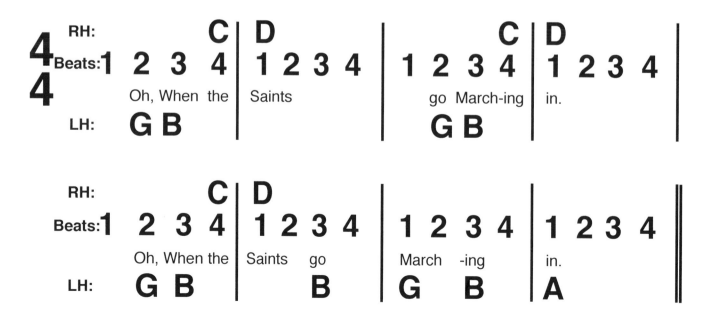

Lesson 28: Chapter 3
What We Have Learned

- Playing with Both Hands

- *Yankee Doodle*

- *When the Saints Go Marching In*

- *Take Me Out to the Ballgame*

- Intervals

- *Ode to Joy*

- Beethoven *5th Symphony Theme*

Check Out These Artists, Songs, and Pieces

- Chopin: *Nocturnes*

- McCoy Tyner: *Giant Steps*

- Lang Lang: *Liszt Concerto #1*

- Lady Gaga: *Speechless*

- Alicia Keys: *Fallin'*

Rhythm & Meter

Chapter 4

Lesson 29: Whole Notes, Half Notes & Quarter Notes

- Let's take a look at some basic rhythms.
- Quarter Notes are notes that get 1 Beat (or Count).
- Half Notes are notes that get 2 Beats (or Counts).
- Whole Notes are notes that get 4 Beats (or Counts).
- In the next 3 examples, try counting on each beat of the 4/4 measures aloud, for example: 1,2,3,4.
- Clap on the quarter, half, and whole notes.

See Video Lesson 6

♩ = 1 Beat   ♩ = 2 Beats   o = 4 Beats

Example 1:
Try Clapping on each "X", while counting the beats.

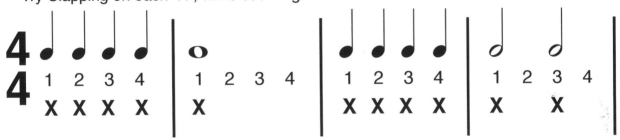

Example 2:
Try Clapping on each "X", while counting the beats.

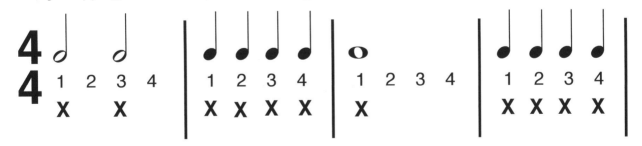

Example 3:
Try Clapping on each "X", while counting the beats.

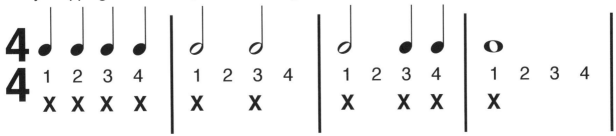

Lesson 30: 5-Note Songs with Half Notes & Quarter Notes

- Try these songs that use Half Notes (2 beats or counts) and quarter notes (1 beat or count).
- All of the songs on this page are for the Right Hand (RH).
- Try to count aloud (1,2,3,4) for each measure.

RH

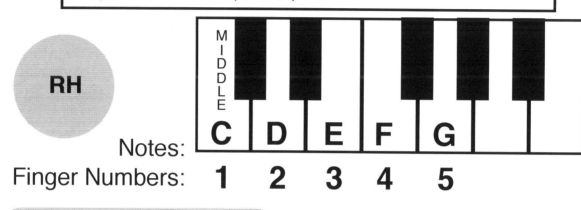

Notes: **C D E F G**

Finger Numbers: **1 2 3 4 5**

See Video Lesson 6

Lyrical Melody

4/4
| G | F | E | C | D | D | D | D | G | F | E | C | D | D | C | C |
Beats: 1 2 3 4 | 1 2 3 4 | 1 2 3 4 | 1 2 3 4

The Bells

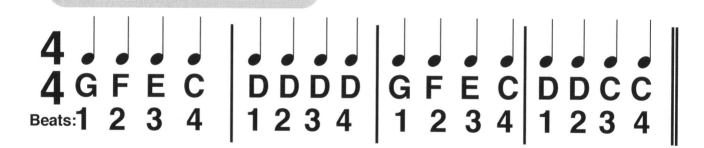

4/4
C (1) ___ G (3) ___ | C (1) ___ G (3) ___ | F E D C (1 2 3 4) | D D G (1 2 3)

Beats: 1 2 3 4 | 1 2 3 4 | 1 2 3 4 | 1 2 3 4

C (1) ___ G (3) ___ | C (1) ___ G (3) ___ | F E D C (1 2 3 4) | D D C (1 2 3)

1 2 3 4 | 1 2 3 4 | 1 2 3 4 | 1 2 3 4

Lesson 31: 5-Note Songs with Half Notes & Quarter Notes

- Try these songs that use Half Notes (2 beats or counts) and Quarter Notes (1 beat or count).
- All of the songs on this page are for the Right Hand (RH).
- Try to count aloud (1,2,3,4) for each measure.

RH

MIDDLE

Notes: C D E F G

Finger Numbers: 1 2 3 4 5

Sunshine

The numbers are for the **beats.**

4
4 G F E C | D D D D | G F E C | D D C C ‖
Beats: 1 2 3 4 | 1 2 3 4 | 1 2 3 4 | 1 2 3 4

On the Beach

4
4 F   C | G   C | F E D C | D D E
Beats: 1 2 3 4 | 1 2 3 4 | 1 2 3 4 | 1 2 3 4

F   C | G   C | F E D C | D D C ‖
1 2 3 4 | 1 2 3 4 | 1 2 3 4 | 1 2 3 4

Lesson 32: 5-Note Songs with Half, Whole, & Quarter Notes

- Try these songs that use Quarter Notes (1 beat), Half Notes (2 beats) and Whole Notes (4 beats).
- All of the songs on this page are for the Right Hand (RH).
- Try to count aloud (1,2,3,4) for each measure.

RH

Notes: **C D E F G**

Finger Numbers: **1 2 3 4 5**

In the Moonlight

The numbers are for the <u>beats.</u>

4/4 o **G** | o **C** | G F E C | D D C C
Beats: 1 2 3 4 | 1 2 3 4 | 1 2 3 4 | 1 2 3 4

First Light

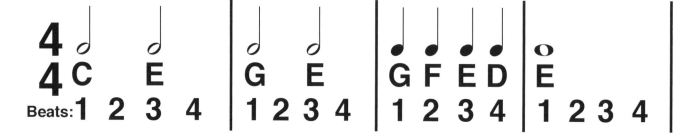

Lesson 33: 5-Note Songs with Half Notes & Quarter Notes

- Try these songs that use Half Notes (2 beats or counts) and quarter notes (1 beat or count).
- All of the songs on this page are for the Left Hand (LH).
- Try to count aloud (1,2,3,4) for each measure.

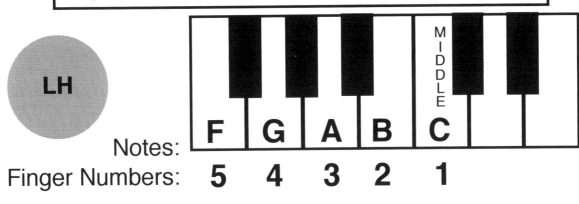

LH

Notes: F G A B C (MIDDLE)

Finger Numbers: 5 4 3 2 1

Autumn Afternoon

The numbers are for the **beats.**

4/4	A	F	C	A	G	G	G	G	A	F	C	A	F	F	F	F
Beats:	1	2	3	4	1	2	3	4	1	2	3	4	1	2	3	4

Golden Bells

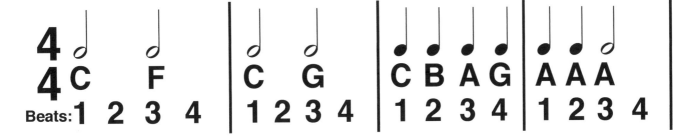

4/4	C		F		C		G		C	B	A	G	A	A	A	
Beats:	1	2	3	4	1	2	3	4	1	2	3	4	1	2	3	4

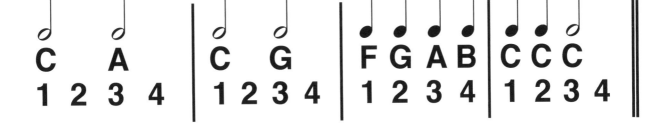

	C		A		C		G		F	G	A	B	C	C	C	
	1	2	3	4	1	2	3	4	1	2	3	4	1	2	3	4

Lesson 34: 5-Note Songs with Half, Whole, & Quarter Notes

- Try these songs that use Quarter Notes (1 beat), Half Notes (2 beats) and Whole Notes (4 beats or counts).
- All of the songs on this page are for the Left Hand (LH).
- Try to count aloud (1,2,3,4) for each measure.

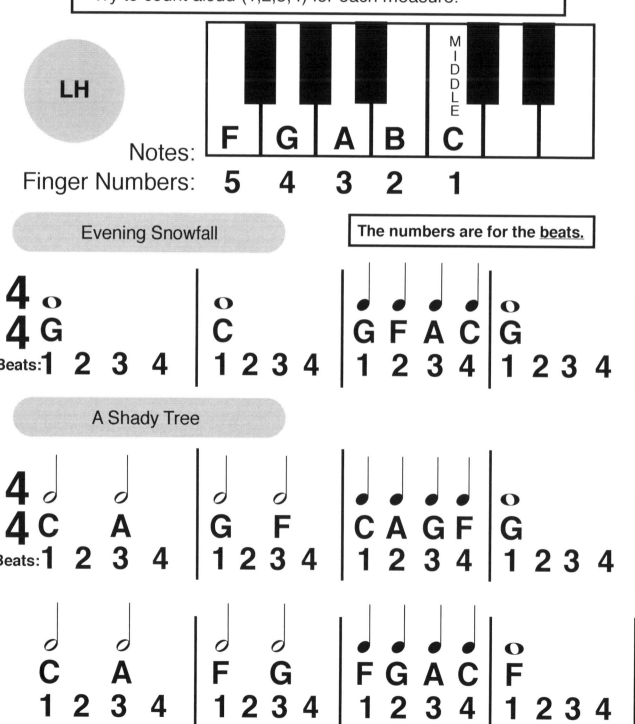

Chapter 4
What We Have Learned

- Whole Notes = 4 Beats = 𝅝
- Half Notes = 2 Beats = 𝅗𝅥
- Quarter Notes = 1 Beat = 𝅘𝅥
- *The Bells*
- *First Light*
- *Evening Snowfall*
- *A Shady Tree*

Check Out These Artists, Songs, and Pieces

- Cold Play: *Clocks*
- Michael Nyman: *Music from the Piano*
- Billy Joel: *Baby Grand*
- J.S. Bach: *Minuet in G*
- Adele: *Turning Tables*

The Treble Clef

Chapter 5

Lesson 35: Treble Clef Notes: Middle C, D, and E

- The Treble Clef mainly is used for notes above Middle C.
- About 90% of the time, it is used for the Right Hand.
  (There are a few occasions in songs or pieces when it is used for the Left Hand.)
- The Treble Clef is made up of Lines and Spaces that correspond to keys on the piano.
  Each Line or Space is linked to <u>one</u> (and only one) key on the piano.
- We will learn more about the lines and spaces of the Treble Clef in the following lessons.

Middle C

This is the TrebleClef Symbol:

Middle C is under the Treble Clef. There is a line through the middle of the note.

Note:

Finger Number: **1**

See Video Lesson 7

D

D is under the Treble Clef, as well. It hangs under the lowest line of the Treble Clef.

Note:

Finger Number: **2**

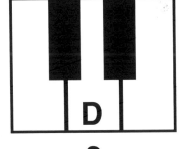

E

E is on the first line of the Treble Clef.

Note:

Finger Number: **3**

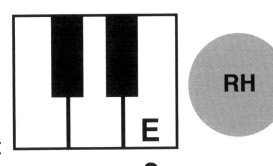

Lesson 36: Treble Clef Songs: Middle C, D, and E (RH)

- Let's play 4 songs with notes of the Treble Clef: C, D, and E.
- Remember to find Middle C with the Thumb of your right hand (RH).

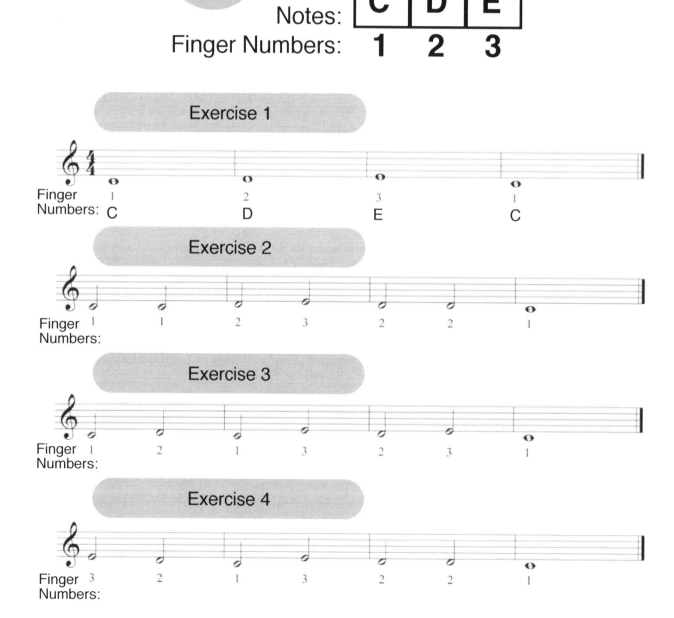

RH

Notes: C D E
Finger Numbers: **1 2 3**

Exercise 1

Finger Numbers: 1 2 3 1
C D E C

Exercise 2

Finger Numbers: 1 1 2 3 2 2 1

Exercise 3

Finger Numbers: 1 2 1 3 2 3 1

Exercise 4

Finger Numbers: 3 2 1 3 2 2 1

Lesson 37: Treble Clef Songs: Middle C, D, E, & F (RH)

- Let's add the note F, which is on the 1st space of the Treble Clef.
- Remember to find Middle C with the Thumb of your right hand (RH).

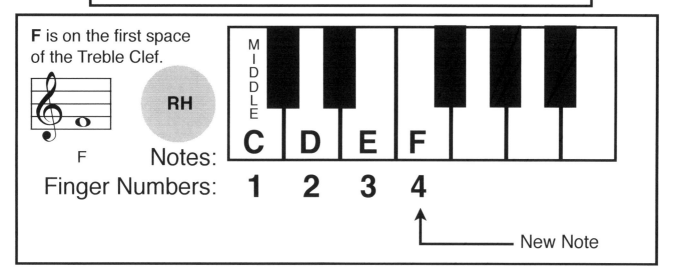

F is on the first space of the Treble Clef.

F

RH

Notes: C D E F

Finger Numbers: **1** **2** **3** **4**

New Note

Exercise 1

Finger Numbers: 3 2 1 2 4 4 3 3 3 2 1 2 4 4 1 1
                              F   F

Exercise 2

Finger Numbers: 1 3 2 4 3 2 1 2 2 1
                        F

Exercise 3

Finger Numbers: 4 3 2 2 3 1 4 3 2 1 2 1

Lesson 38: The Treble Clef: Lines Overview

- Each line of the Treble Clef stands for a specific note and key on the piano.
- The lines have numbers that go from 1 to 5. Line 1 is the lowest line. Line 5 is the top line (or highest line) on the Treble Clef.
- To help you remember the note names of each line, memorize the saying below. In the saying ("Every Good Bird Does Fly"). "Every" stands for "E", "Good" stands for "G", "Bird" stands for "B", "Does" stands for "D", and "Fly" stands for "F".
- The "E" of "Every" stands for the "E" piano key 2 notes above Middle C. See the charts below to better understand these notes. **See Video Lesson 7**

From bottom to top, this is the pattern for the lines: E, G, B, D, F

Line Numbers

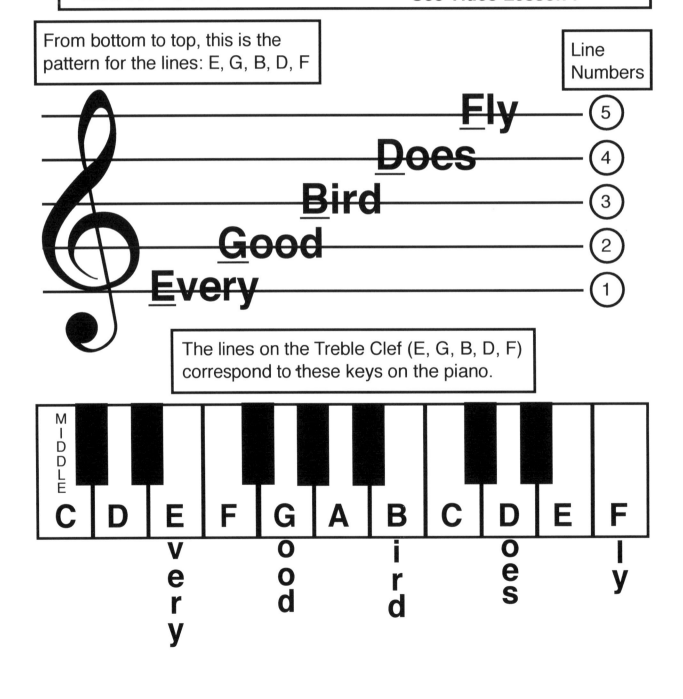

The lines on the Treble Clef (E, G, B, D, F) correspond to these keys on the piano.

Lesson 39: The Treble Clef: Spaces Overview

- Each space of the Treble Clef stands for a specific note and key on the piano.
- The spaces have numbers that go from 1 to 4. Space 1 is the lowest space. Space 4 is the top space (or highest space) on the Treble Clef.
- To help you learn the note names of each space, remember that the spaces of the Treble Clef form the word "Face" spelled upside down (from bottom space to top.)
- The "F" of "Face" stands for the "F" piano key 4 notes above Middle C.
- See the charts below to better understand the other notes. **See Video Lesson 7**

From bottom to top, this is the pattern for the Spaces: F, A, C, E

Space Numbers

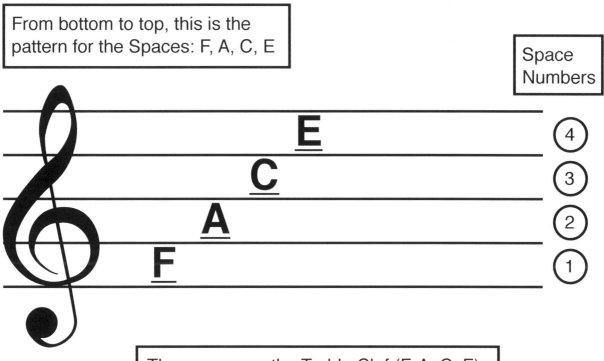

The spaces on the Treble Clef (F, A, C, E) correspond to these keys on the piano.

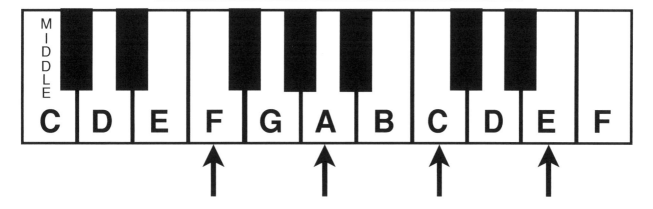

Lesson 40: Kum-Bah-Yah: New Notes: G and A

- Let's add 2 new notes G and A, which are on the 2nd line and space of the Treble Clef.
- Remember to find Middle C with the Thumb of your right hand (RH).

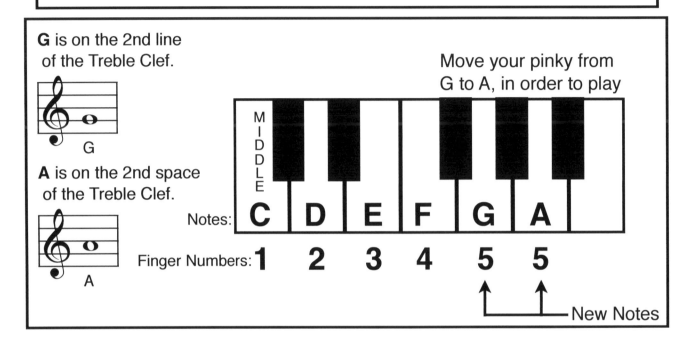

G is on the 2nd line of the Treble Clef.

G

A is on the 2nd space of the Treble Clef.

A

Move your pinky from G to A, in order to play

Notes: **C D E F G A**

Finger Numbers: **1 2 3 4 5 5**

New Notes

Kum-Bah-Yah

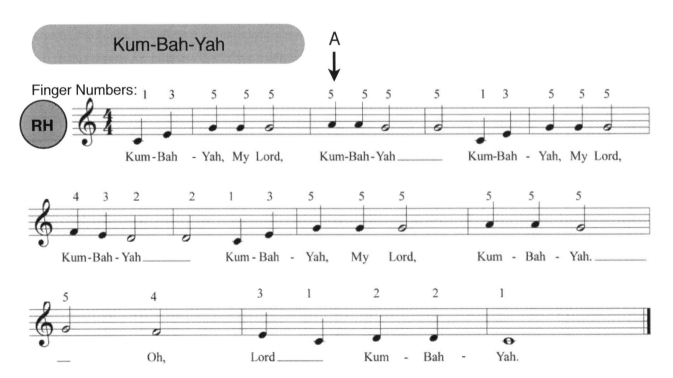

Finger Numbers:

RH

1 3   5   5   5   5   5   5   5   1 3   5   5   5

Kum-Bah - Yah, My Lord,   Kum-Bah-Yah_____   Kum-Bah - Yah, My Lord,

4 3 2   2   1   3   5   5   5   5   5   5

Kum-Bah - Yah_____   Kum - Bah - Yah, My Lord,   Kum - Bah - Yah._____

5   4   3   1   2   2   1

___   Oh,   Lord_____   Kum - Bah - Yah.

Chapter 5
What We Have Learned

- Treble Clef Keys: C, D, E, F, and G

- *Kum-Bah-Yah*

- Treble Clef Lines

- Treble Clef Spaces

- 3-Note Treble Clef Songs

- 4-Note Treble Clef Songs

- 5-Note Treble Clef Songs

Check Out These Artists, Songs, and Pieces

- John Legend: *Ordinary People*

- C.P.E. Bach: *Solfeggietto*

- Ben Folds Five: *Brick*

- Ligeti: *Piano Etudes*

- Greyson Chance: *Waiting Outside the Lines*

The Bass Clef

Chapter 6

Lesson 41: The Bass Clef, Middle C, B, and A

- The Bass Clef mainly is used for notes below Middle C.
- About 90% of the time, it is used for the Left Hand.
  (There are a few occasions in songs when it is used for the Right Hand.)
- The word "Bass" is pronounced like the word "Base" (as in "Baseball").
- The Bass Clef is made up of Lines and Spaces that correspond to keys on the piano.
  Each Line or Space is linked to <u>one</u> (and only one) key on the piano.
- We will learn more about the lines and spaces of the Bass Clef in the following lessons.

Middle C

This is the
Bass Clef
Symbol: 𝄢

Middle C is above the Bass Clef. There is a line through the middle of the note.

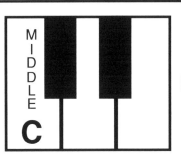

Note:

Finger Number: **1**

B

B is on the Bass Clef. It sits on top of the highest line of the Bass Clef.

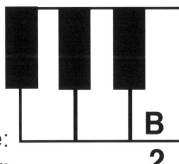

Note:

Finger Number: **2**

A

A is on the fifth line of the Bass Clef.

Note:

Finger Number: **3**

Lesson 42: The Bass Clef
A, B and Middle C

- Let's play 4 songs with notes of the Bass Clef: A, B, and C.
- Remember to find Middle C with the Thumb of your left hand (LH).

LH

Notes: **A** **B** **C** (MIDDLE)

Finger Numbers: **3** **2** **1**

Try saying the notes aloud as you play each song.

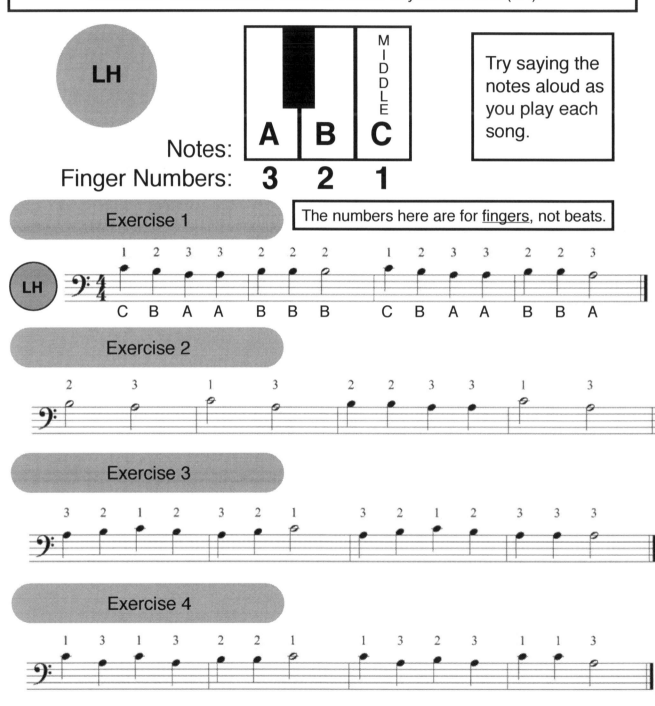

Exercise 1

The numbers here are for <u>fingers</u>, not beats.

| 1 | 2 | 3 | 3 | 2 | 2 | 2 | | 1 | 2 | 3 | 3 | 2 | 2 | 3 |
C | B | A | A | B | B | B | | C | B | A | A | B | B | A

Exercise 2

Exercise 3

Exercise 4

Lesson 43: The Bass Clef
G, A, B and Middle C

- Let's add the note G, which is on the 4th space of the Bass Clef.
- Remember to find Middle C with the Thumb of your right hand (LH).

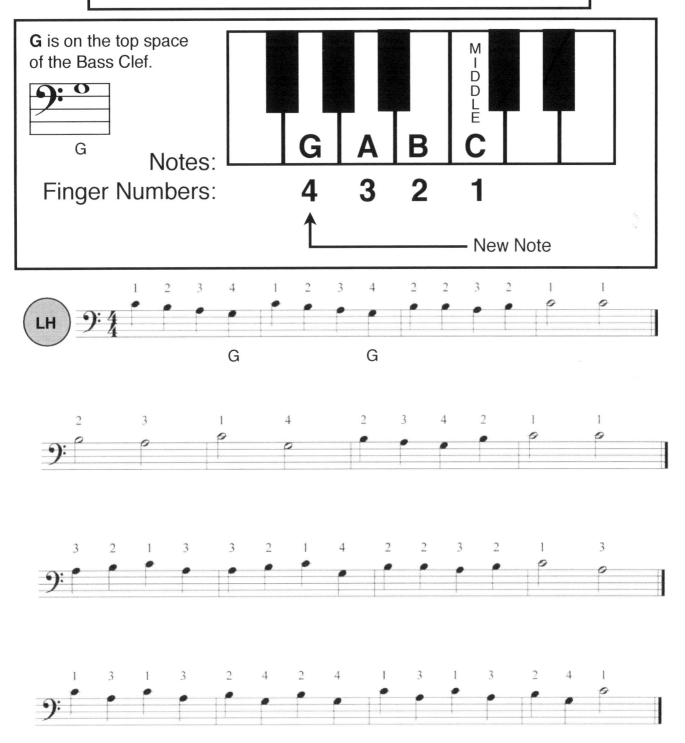

Lesson 44: The Bass Clef: Lines Overview

- Each line of the Bass Clef stands for a specific note and key on the piano.
- The lines have numbers that go from 1 to 5. Line 1 is the lowest line. Line 5 is the top line (or highest line) on the Bass Clef.
- To help you remember the note names of each line, memorize the saying below. In the saying ("Good Baked Desserts For All"). "Good" stands for "G", "Baked" stands for "B", "Desserts" stands for "D", "For" stands for "F", and "All" stands for "A".
- The "A" of "All" stands for the "A" piano key 2 notes below Middle C. See the charts below to better understand these notes. **See Video Lesson 8**

From bottom to top, this is the pattern for the lines: G, B, D, F, A

Line Numbers

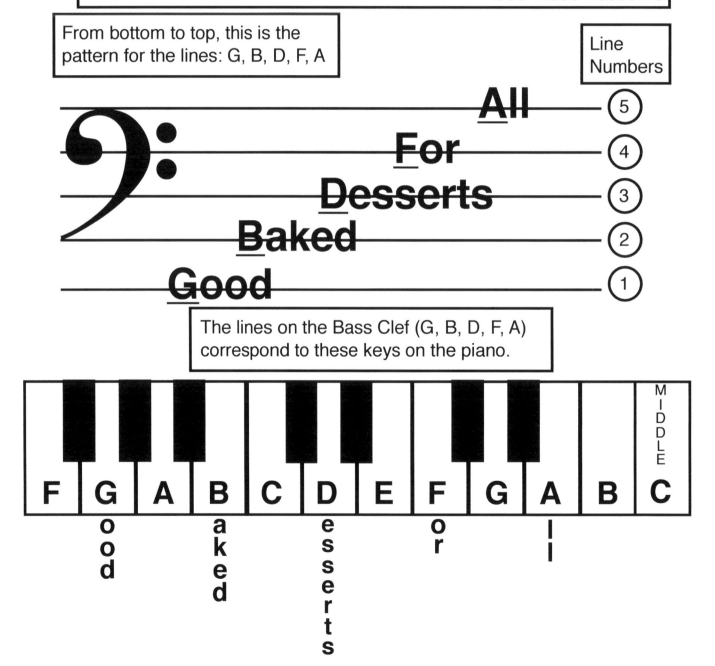

The lines on the Bass Clef (G, B, D, F, A) correspond to these keys on the piano.

Lesson 45: The Bass Clef: Spaces Overview

- Each space of the Bass Clef stands for a specific note and key on the piano.
- The spaces have numbers that go from 1 to 4. Space 1 is the lowest space. Space 4 is the top space (or highest space) on the Bass Clef.
- To help you learn the note names of each space, remember that the spaces of the Bass Clef form the phrase "All cows eat grass".
- The word "All" stands for the key and note "A"; the word "Cows" stands for "C".
- See the charts below to better understand the other notes.

See Video Lesson 8

Space Numbers

Grass ④

Eat ③

Cows ②

All ①

The spaces on the Bass Clef (A, C, E, G) correspond to these keys on the piano.

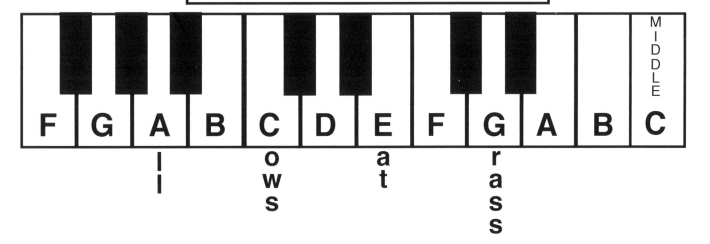

Lesson 46: The Bass Clef Songs: F, G, A, B, and Middle C

- Let's add the note F, which is on the 4th line of the Bass Clef.
- Remember to find Middle C with the Thumb of your left hand (LH).

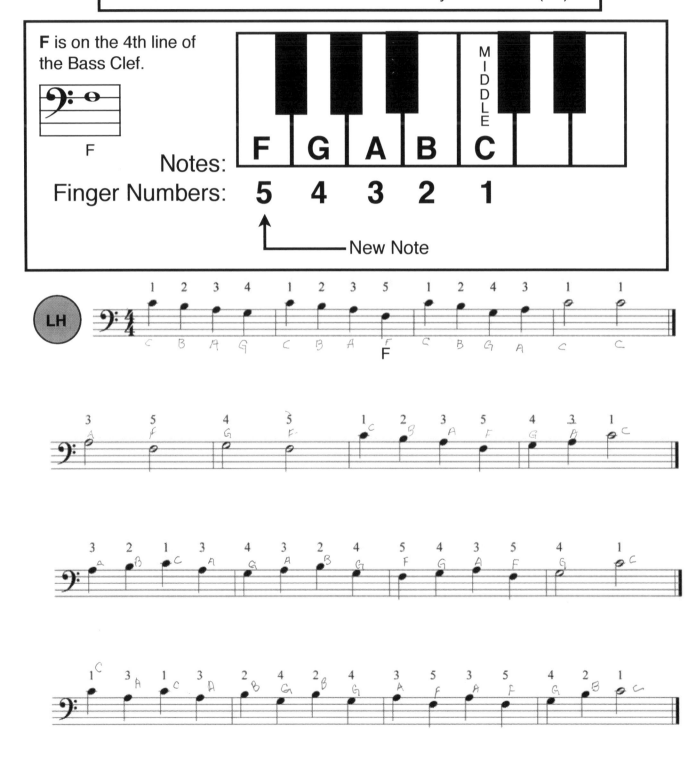

Lesson 47: The Bass Clef Songs: F, G, A, B, and Middle C

- Let's add the note F, which is on the 4th line of the Bass Clef.
- Remember to find Middle C with the Thumb of your left hand (LH).

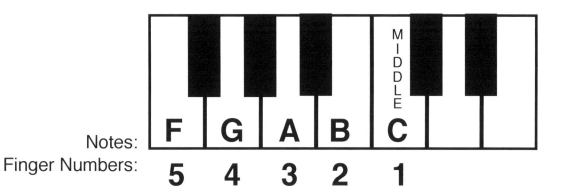

Notes: F G A B C
Finger Numbers: 5 4 3 2 1

Exercise 1

Exercise 2

Exercise 3

Exercise 4

Lesson 48: Chapter 6
What We Have Learned

- Bass Clef Keys: F, G, A, B, and Middle C

- Bass Clef Lines

- Bass Clef Spaces

- 3-Note Bass Clef Songs

- 4-Note Treble Clef Songs

- 5-Note Treble Clef Songs

Check Out These Artists, Songs, and Pieces

- The Fray: *How to Save a Life*

- Thelonius Monk: *Round Midnight*

- Sara Bareilles: *Love Song*

- Dave Brubeck: *Take Five*

- Chopin: *Revolutionary Etude*

The Grand Staff

Chapter 7

Lesson 49: The Grand Staff Overview

- The Grand Staff is formed by combining the Treble and Bass Clefs.
- All of the rules that we have learned so far about both clefs are still true for the Grand Staff. Using the Grand Staff makes it easier to read music written for both hands.
- Study the chart below to understand how the Staff works. **See Video Lesson 9**

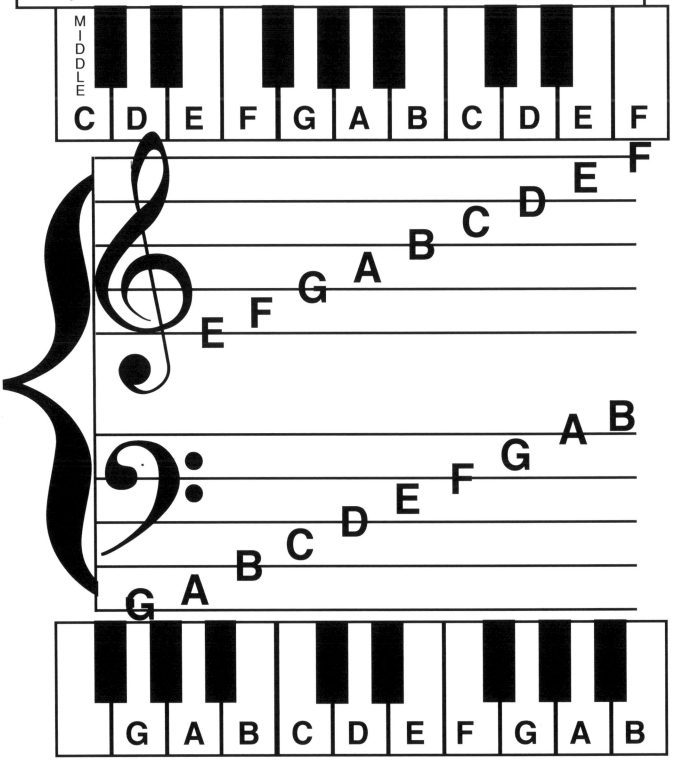

Lesson 50: *Simple Gifts*

Lesson 51: Amazing Grace

Amazing Grace is in 3/4 Time. Remember to count "One, Two, Three" for each measure.

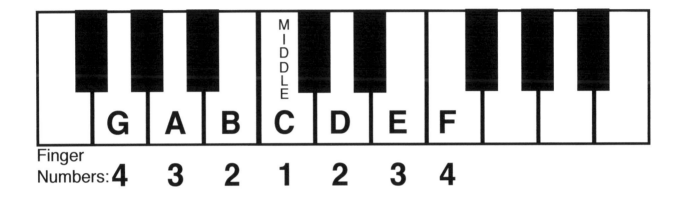

Finger Numbers: **4 3 2 1 2 3 4**

Amazing Grace

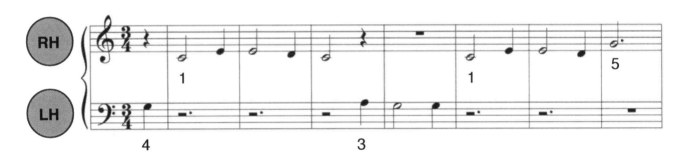

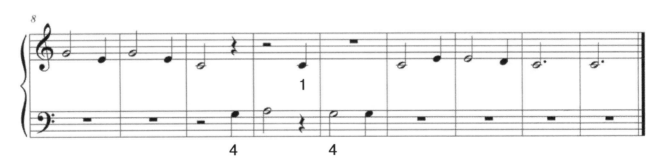

Lesson 52:
Michael, Row the Boat Ashore

Michael, Row the Boat Ashore is in 4/4 Time. Remember to count "One, Two, Three, Four" for each measure.

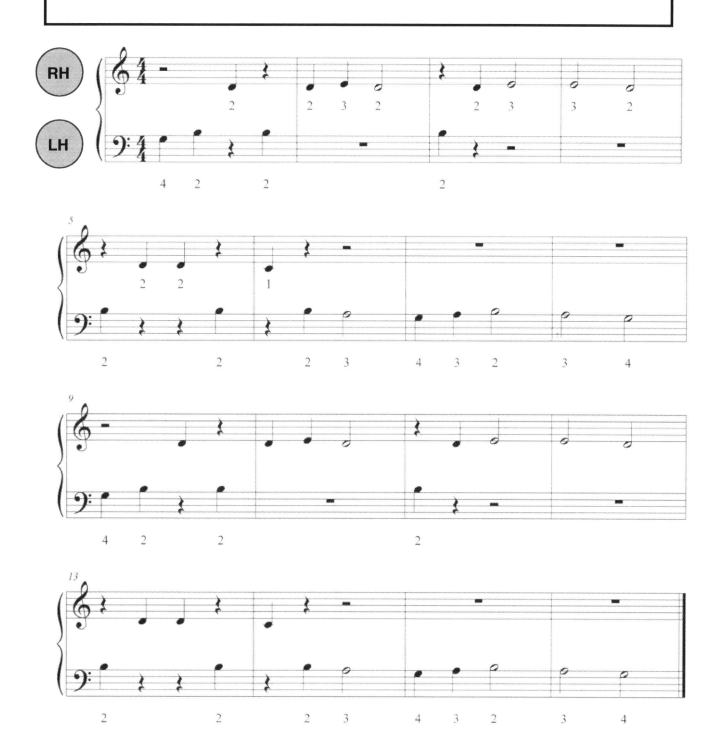

Lesson 53:
In May

- Slurs (or Phrase Markers) are curved lines that go over or under two or more different notes in piano music.
- They indicate two things: to play a passage or phrase with a smooth sound ("legato", which means smooth or connected notes played) and slurs (or phrase markers) also indicate where a musical phrase (the musical equivalent to a sentence) starts and ends.

A Slur (or Phrase Marker)
looks like this: ⟶

Lesson 54:
Scarborough Fair

• *Scarborough Fair* is in 3/4 Time. Count: One, Two, Three
• For the F#, play the black key directly to the right of F on the piano.

Scarborough Fair

Lesson 55: Chapter 7
What We Have Learned

- The Grand Staff

- *Simple Gifts*

- *Amazing Grace*

- *Michael, Row the Boat Ashore*

- *In May*

- *Scarborough Fair*

Check Out These Artists, Songs, and Pieces

- Art Tatum: *Someone to Watch Over Me*

- Brahms: *Piano Concerto #2*

- Duke Ellington: *Take the A Train*

- The Beatles: *Hey Jude*

- Keith Jarrett: *Over the Rainbow*

Easy Chords

Chapter 8

Lesson 56: Easy Chords
C Major, F Major, & G7

- Chords are 3 or more notes played at the same time.
- In order to play chords well, keep your fingers curved for the notes that you play and lift your fingers that are not being used for the chord.
- Take a look at video lesson 10 to see and hear how these techniques work.
- For these chords, use the Left Hand (LH).
- We are going to look at 3 chords in this lesson.

See Video Lesson 10

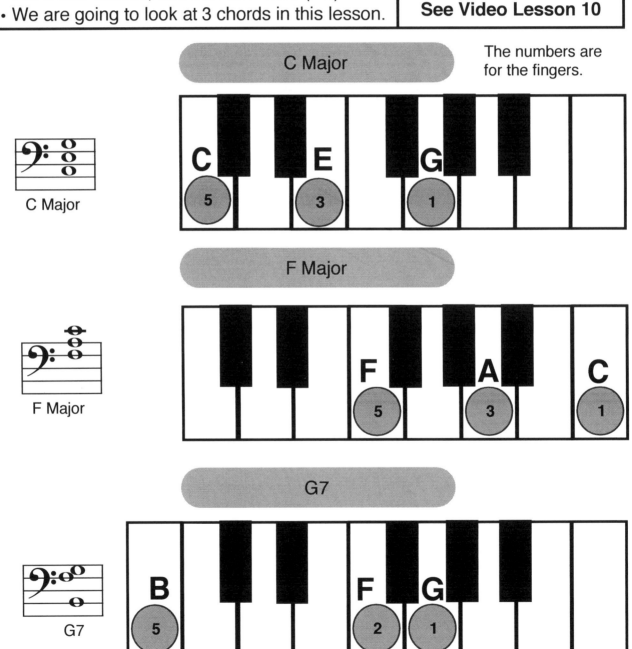

The numbers are for the fingers.

Lesson 57: *Chord Dance*
C Major & G7 Chords

• *Chord Dance* is in 4/4 Time. There are 4 beats per measure.
• The song has C Major and G7 chords.

Lesson 58: *Ode to Joy,* Chord Version

- This version of *Ode to Joy* uses the C Major and G7 Chords.
- Remember to count the beats as you play.
- The piece is in 4/4 Time: 4 Beats per measure.

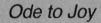

Ode to Joy

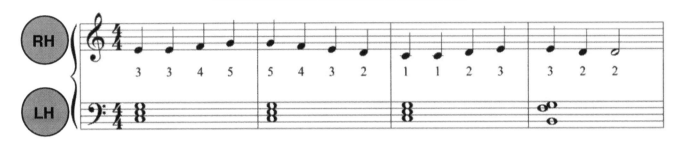

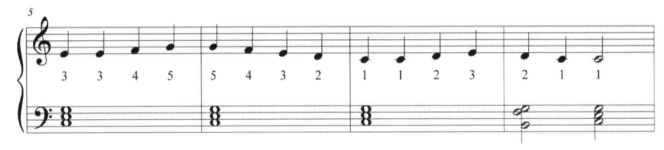

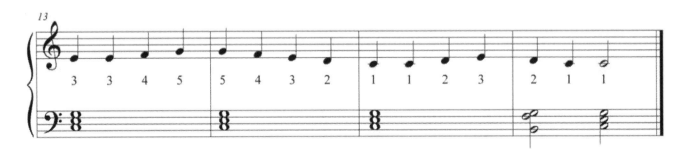

Lesson 59: Easy Chords
A Minor, D Minor, & G Major

- Let's look at 3 more chords for the Left Hand: A Minor, D Minor, & G Major.
- Make sure to keep your fingers curved and lift the fingers that do not play.

See Video Lesson 10

The numbers are for the fingers.

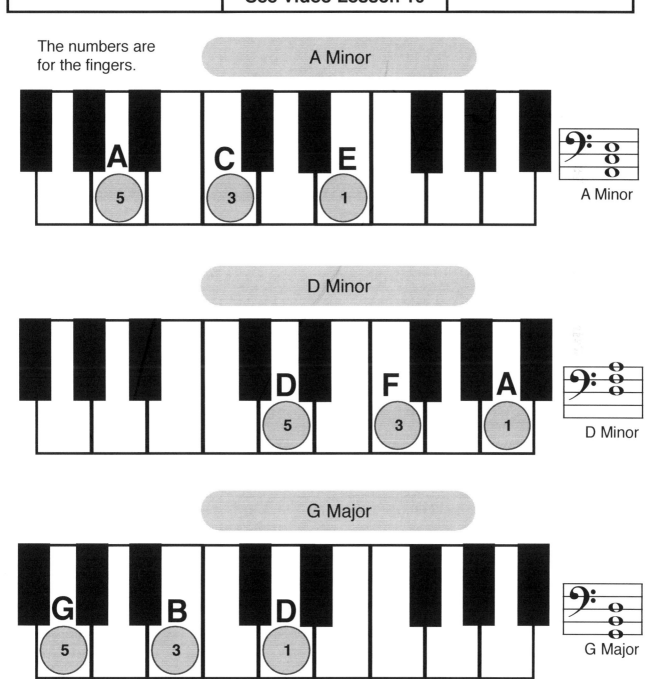

Lesson 60:
Jazz Dance

- *Jazz Dance* is in 4/4 Time (4 Beats per Measure).
- The melody has quarter notes and half notes.
- The chords are in the left hand.
- The melody is in the right hand.
- Play the chords on the first beat of each measure.

Chapter 8
What We Have Learned

- Easy Chords

- C Major Chord

- G7 Chord

- F Major Chord

- A Minor Chord

- D7 Chord

- E7 Chord

Check Out These Artists, Songs, and Pieces

- Queen: *Bohemian Rhapsody*

- Chopin: *Preludes*

- Eric Clapton: *Layla*

- Liszt: *Transcendental Etudes*

- Frank Sinatra: *New York, New York*

Music Theory & Piano Technique

Chapter 9
Bonus Lessons

Lesson 61: Music Theory
What are Sharps & Flats?

- On the piano, there are two types of keys: Black Keys and White Keys.
- The White Keys stand for natural notes, for example, C, D, E, F, G, A and B.
- The Black Keys (also called "accidentals") stand for Sharp or Flat Notes.
- Sharp Notes use this symbol: #
- Flat Notes use this symbol: ♭
- Here are some examples of Sharp Notes: F#, G#, A#, C#, D#
- Here are some examples of Flat Notes: Gb, Ab, Bb, Db, Eb

- On the piano keyboard, Sharp Keys are located directly to the right of their corresponding Natural Key (White Key). For example, F Sharp (F#) is the next key to the right from F (also called "F Natural"). C Sharp (C#) is the black key directly to the right of C (also called "C Natural").
- This pattern, of going to the next key directly to the right, holds true for all of the sharp notes going up and down the piano keyboard.
- Using the chart below, try locating the following sharp keys on the piano: C#, F#, D#, A#, G#.

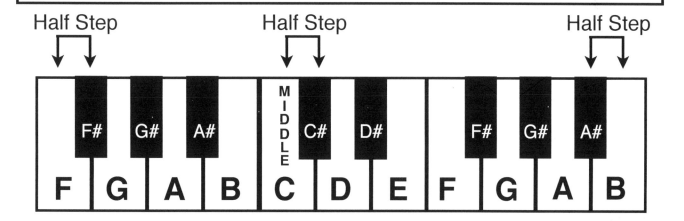

- The distance from a White Key to a Black Key, for example, F to F#, C to C#, or A# to B, is called a **Half Step** or Minor Second. **Remember this.** It is a bit of important information we will be referring to many times in the next book.

Lesson 62: Music Theory More on Flats and Sharps

- On the piano keyboard, Flat Keys are located directly to the left of their corresponding Natural Key (White Key). For example, G Flat (Gb) is the next black key to the left from G (also called "G Natural"). E Flat (Eb) is the black key directly to the left of E (also called "E Natural").
- This pattern, of going to the next key directly to the left, holds true for all of the flat notes going up and down the piano keyboard.
- Using the chart below, try locating the following flat keys on the piano: Ab, Db, Gb, Eb, Bb. **Remember: This pattern is the same for the entire keyboard.**

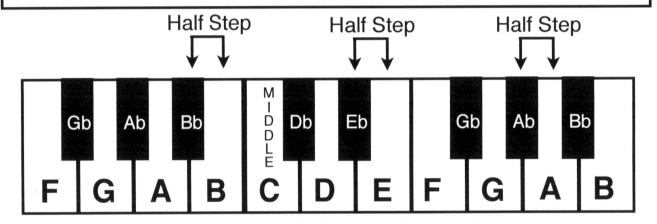

- The distance (up or down) from a White Key to a Black Key, for example, from B to Bb, Eb to E, or A to Ab, is called a Half Step or Minor Second. See Above.

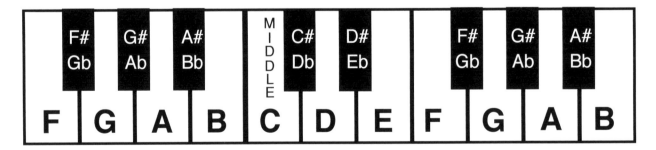

- You might have noticed in the last two lessons that there are 2 names for each Black Key: A Sharp Name and a Flat Name. This is true for the entire piano.
- Depending on the musical context (which we will learn more about throughout this book), a black key may be called by either its sharp or flat name. For example, A Flat and G Sharp are the same key on the piano; C Sharp and D Flat are the same key; and F Sharp and G Flat are the same key. See Above.

Lesson 63: Music Theory
What is a Scale?

- Scales are groups of notes that are arranged in stepwise patterns, either going up or going down. The combination of these steps (also called "Intervals") gives each type of scale its unique sound and character.
- Throughout this book, we are going to learn the specifics for each type of scale, for instance, Major Scales, Minor Scales, Modes, Chromatic, etc.
- Most scales are made up of Half Steps and Whole Steps.
- A Half Step (also called "Minor Second" Interval) is the distance from one piano key to the very next piano key, for example, from C to C# (white key to black key) or from E to F. In both cases, there are no keys (whether white keys or black keys) between those two notes.
- Whole Steps (also called "Major Second" Intervals), are made up of two Half Steps. For example, C to D is a whole step: 2 Half Steps combined--C to C# and then C# to D. See Chart Below.

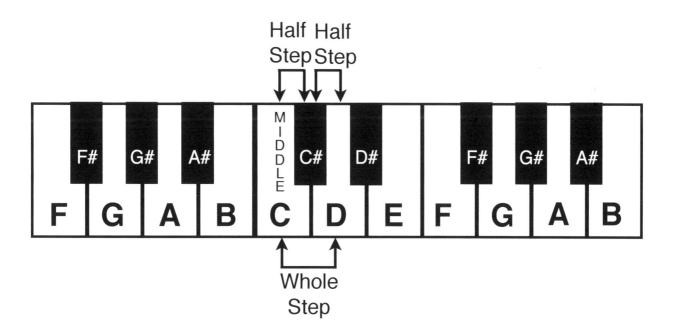

- Here are some other examples of Whole Steps: G to A, E to D, B to C#, F to G.
- Try playing the following Whole Steps (going up or down) and listen to their sound characteristics: A to B, C# to D#, A to G, F# to G#. Use the chart above to help you locate the notes. Listen to the similarities between each group.

Lesson 64: Music Theory
What is a Major Scale?

- All Major Scales follow the same pattern of whole steps and half steps.
- All Major Scales have 8 notes. For example, here are the notes of the C Major Scale: C, D, E, F, G, A, B, C. There are 8 notes (or keys) total.
- The Pattern for all Major Scales, Ascending (going up on the keyboard), is: 2 Whole Steps, 1 Half Step, 3 Whole Steps, then 1 Half Step.
- In the 2 diagrams below, take a look at the pattern of Whole Steps and Half Steps. Try playing the C Major Scale (shown below) and listen to the steps.

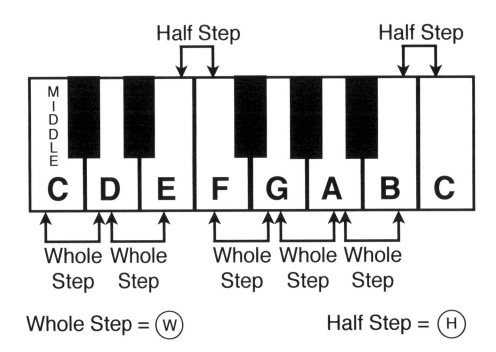

Whole Step = (W)   Half Step = (H)

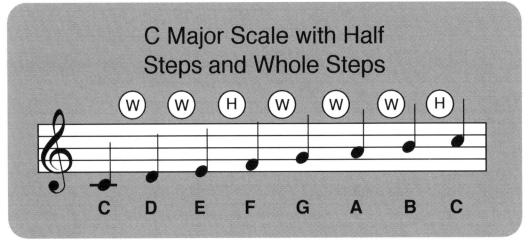

C Major Scale with Half Steps and Whole Steps

Lesson 65: 5-Finger Scales C, G, and D Major: Right Hand

- In these 3 exercises, we will be playing the first 5 notes of the C, D, and G Major Scales in the Right Hand. Remember to keep your fingers curved as you play. After you practice these patterns 10 times. **Have Fun!**

C Major

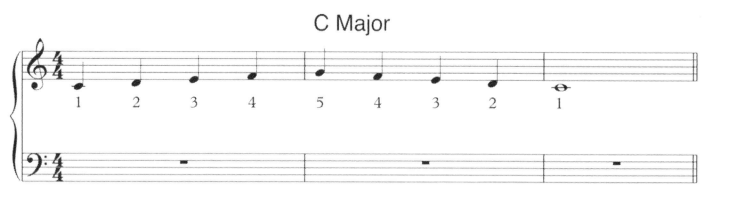

G Major

The Sharps are added here to help.

D Major

Lesson 66: 5-Finger Scales C, G, and D Major: Left Hand

• In these 3 exercises, we will be playing the first 5 notes of the C, D, and G Major Scales in the Left Hand. Remember to keep your fingers curved as you play. After you practice these patterns 10 times. **Have Fun!**

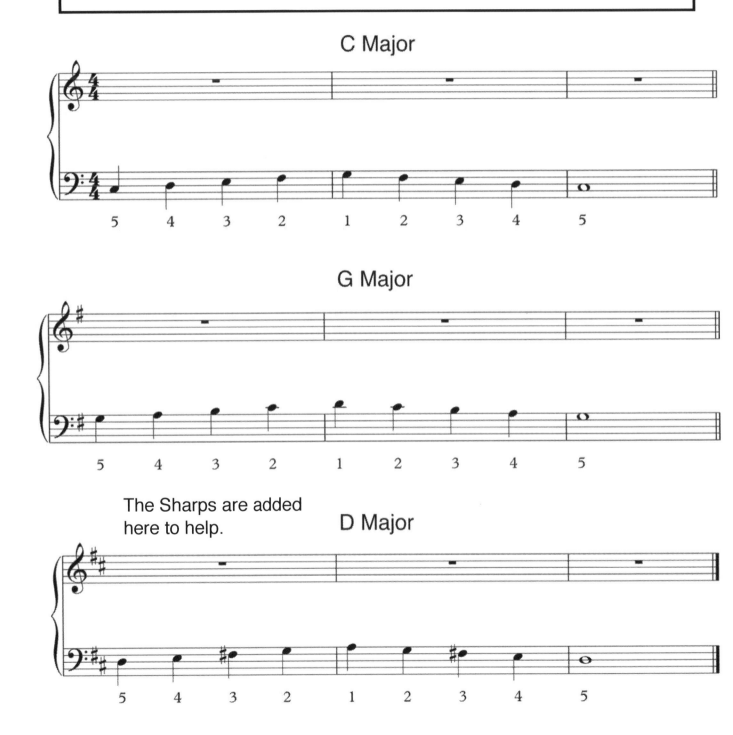

C Major

5   4   3   2   1   2   3   4   5

G Major

5   4   3   2   1   2   3   4   5

The Sharps are added here to help.

D Major

5   4   3   2   1   2   3   4   5

Lesson 67: 5-Finger Scales
C, G, and D Major: Both Hands

- In these 3 exercises, we will be playing the first 5 notes of the C, D, and G Major Scales in Both Hands. Remember to keep your fingers curved as you play.

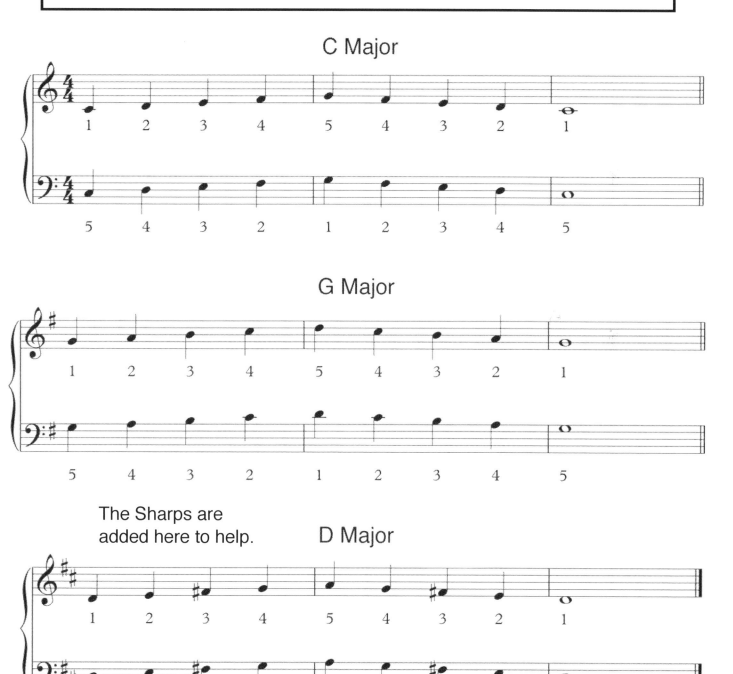

C Major

G Major

The Sharps are added here to help.　　　D Major

Lesson 68: 5-Finger Scales A, E, and B Major: Right Hand

• In these 3 exercises, we will be playing the first 5 notes of the A, E, and B Major Scales in the Right Hand. Play each exercise ten times.

The Sharps are added here to help.

A Major

1   2   3   4   5   4   3   2   1

E Major

1   2   3   4   5   4   3   2   1

B Major

1   2   3   4   5   4   3   2   1

Lesson 69: 5-Finger Scales A, E, and B Major: Left Hand

• In these 3 exercises, we will be playing the first 5 notes of the A, E, and B Major Scales in the Left Hand. Play each exercise ten times.

The Sharps are added
here to help.

Lesson 70: 5-Finger Scales A, E, and B Major: Both Hands

• In these 3 exercises, we will be playing the first 5 notes of the A, E, and B Major Scales in Both Hands. Play each exercise ten times.

The Sharps are added
here to help.

A Major

E Major

B Major

Congratulations!
You have completed the Book!

Great work in completing this book and video course on the basics of piano. You now have an understanding of the fundamentals of piano playing: basic piano technique, beginner-level note reading and chord playing, a repertoire of songs and pieces to perform for family and friends, and some understanding of music fundamentals--such as time signatures, beats, and the grand staff.

Keep up the good work and continue to practice and play the piano!

Damon Ferrante

If you enjoyed this book, please recommend the paperback edition to your local library.

Damon Ferrante is a composer, guitarist, and professor of piano studies. He has taught on the music faculties of Seton Hall University and Montclair State University. For over 20 years, Damon has taught guitar, piano, composition, and music theory. Damon has had performances at Carnegie Hall, Symphony Space, and throughout the US and Europe. His main teachers have been David Rakowski at Columbia University, Stanley Wolfe at Juilliard, and Bruno Amato at the Peabody Conservatory of Johns Hopkins University. Damon has written two operas, a guitar concerto, song cycles, orchestral music, and numerous solo and chamber music works. He has over 30 music books and scores in print. For more information on his books and music, please visit steeplechasmusic.com.

Learn Guitar!

Guitar Adventures
Book & Streaming Videos
for Beginners

New Edition with 101 Lessons!

Damon Ferrante
Fun, Informative & Step-By-Step, Lesson Guide to Guitar,
Beginner & Intermediate Levels (Book & Streaming Videos)

Guitar Adventures
for Kids

Book & Videos, Level 1   Damon Ferrante

Made in the USA
Lexington, KY
03 August 2016